D0122311

PIRATES
AND
PRIVATEERS
OF THE
HIGH SEAS

The *Collective Biographies* Series

African-American Poets
0-89490-774-3

AIDS
Ten Stories of Courage
0-89490-766-2

American Revolutionaries and
Founders of the Nation
0-7660-1115-1

American Astronomers
0-89490-631-3

American Civil Rights Leaders
0-7660-1381-2

American Computer Pioneers
0-7660-1053-8

American Dinosaur Hunters
0-89490-710-7

American Environmental Heroes
0-89490-630-5

American Generals of World War II
0-7660-1024-4

American Heroes of Exploration
and Flight
0-89490-619-4

American Horror Writers
0-7660-1379-0

American Inventors of
the 20th Century
0-89490-632-1

American Jazz Musicians
0-7660-1027-9

American Legends of Rock
0-89490-709-3

American Science Fiction
and Fantasy Writers
0-7660-1090-2

American Tycoons
0-7660-1112-7

American Women Against Violence
0-7660-1025-2

American Writers of the 20th Century
0-89490-704-2

Asian American Authors
0-7660-1376-6

Confederate Generals of the Civil War
0-7660-1029-5

Congressional Medal of Honor Winners
0-7660-1026-0

Great American Businesswomen
0-89490-706-9

Holocaust Rescuers
Ten Stories of Courage
0-7660-1114-3

Legends of American Dance
and Choreography
0-7660-1378-2

Oceanographers and Explorers
of the Sea
0-7660-1113-5

Presidential Medal of Freedom Winners
0-89490-705-0

Scientists of the Ancient World
0-7660-1111-9

Ten Terrific Authors for Teens
0-7660-1380-4

Trailblazing American Women
First in Their Fields
0-7660-1377-4

Union Generals of the Civil War
0-7660-1028-7

Women in America's Wars
0-89490-553-8

Collective Biographies

PIRATES AND PRIVATEERS OF THE HIGH SEAS

Laura Lee Wren

Enslow Publishers, Inc.

40 Industrial Road	PO Box 38
Box 398	Aldershot
Berkeley Heights, NJ 07922	Hants GU12 6BP
USA	UK

http://www.enslow.com

Dedication

For my writers' group; Anna, Elaine, Gary, Lisa, and especially Sue for our many trips to the University Library. You allowed me to plunder your wonderful treasures—your expertise, support and friendship—which kept me afloat. Thank you!

–Laura Lee

Copyright © 2003 by Laura Lee Wren

Library of Congress Cataloging-in-Publication Data

Wren, Laura Lee.
    Pirates and privateers of the high seas / Laura Lee Wren.
        p.cm. – (Collective biographies)
Summary : Describes the lives of the pirates Sir Francis Drake, Sir Henry Morgan, Henry Avery, Samuel Bellamy, Edward Teach, Anne Bonny, Mary Read, Bartholomew Roberts, John Paul Jones, Jean Laffite, and Cheng I Sao.
Includes bibliographical references and index.
    ISBN 0-7660-1542-4
    1. Pirates—Juvenile literature. [1. Pirates.] I. Title. II. Series.
G535 .W74 2002
910.4'5—dc21

2002006617

Printed in the United States of America

10 9 8 7 6 5 4 3 2 1

To Our Readers:
We have done our best to make sure all Internet addresses in this book were active and appropriate when we went to press. However, the author and the publisher have no control over and assume no liability for the material available on those Internet sites or on other Web sites they may link to. Any comments or suggestions can be sent by e-mail to comments@enslow.com or to the address on the back cover.

Every effort has been made to locate all copyright holders of material used in this book. If any errors or omissions have occurred, corrections will be made in future editions of this book.

Illustration Credits: Collectiones . . . Americae pars VII (1599), p. 13; Corel Corporation, pp. 10, 38; Department of Rare Books, New York Public Library, pp. 46; Dover Publications (1837), pp. 33, 46; Enslow Publishers, 14, 23, 28, 56, 67, 78, 80, 86; General History of Pyrates (1725), p. 60; Graphic Maps p. 6; Ken Kinkor/Expedition Whydah, p. 36; U.S. Department of Defense, pp. 70, 74.

Cover Illustration: Ken Kinkor/Expedition Whydah

Contents

In the winter months many pirates sailed the seas in the Caribbean.

Preface

Piracy, the act of robbery on the high seas, has been around since the late 700s, when Vikings terrorized western European coasts and waters. The years between 1690 and 1720, however, are considered the Golden Age of Piracy. Then, thousands of pirates sailed the warm tropical seas of the Caribbean in the winter and headed north during the summer.

They took their stolen loot to the new colonies up and down the American coasts. At first, the colonists welcomed the thriving business, but soon they became victims of pirate attacks themselves. Years later, pirates raided the seas from the coasts of Africa, where they plundered ivory, gold, and slaves, to the coasts of China.

Little is known of the pirates' lives, but their years of piracy have been recorded. The pirates included in this book were all leaders with strong personalities. Like Sir Francis Drake and John Paul Jones, most of them didn't think of themselves as pirates. Instead, they saw themselves as privateers, on a mission for their government. The government would issue a *letter of marque* to the privateer, which allowed him to attack enemy ships. The government would receive a percentage of the treasure. The remainder belonged to the privateer.

Many of the privateers' adventures, however, eventually turned into the cruel raidings of a pirate. Sir

Henry Morgan thought nothing of boarding ships or attacking coastal villages to plunder and take prisoners.

Most pirates grew up in towns near a bustling seaport. There they heard tales of adventures found in a life at sea. By their twenties, most were experienced seamen. Though the life of a pirate promised excitement, it was also a tough way to make a living.

A pirate might hope one day to live off the riches of his plunder, as did Henry Avery and smuggler Jean Laffite. It was more likely, however, that the pirate would suffer the fate of Samuel Bellamy, who sailed into a storm and drowned. Or the pirate might be struck down in battle like Blackbeard and Bartholomew Roberts, or be tried for piracy and hanged.

Men weren't the only villains. Though uncommon, there were some women who emerged as leaders of bands of pirates. Anne Bonny, Mary Read, and Cheng I Sao all fought alongside the men in bloody battles.

A romanticism surrounds those who lived as pirates in the past. Perhaps this is due to the exotic places they traveled. Unfortunately, the violence of piracy is still alive today. "Years ago, [pirates] would steal the cargo, loot the ship's safe and rob the crewmen," said a manager of the International Maritime Bureau. "These days the pirates . . . steal the entire ship and they kill the crew."[1]

Famous pirates of the past became popular figures because of fiction. The names Long John Silver and *Peter Pan*'s Captain Hook are more recognizable today than Henry Avery or even Blackbeard. Whether they are thought of as cruel villains, patriotic heroes, or both, these real pirates led fascinating, dramatic lives that rival those in the movies or in fiction.

In the pages ahead, you will meet some of history's most interesting pirates, the well-known robbers of the high seas.

A seaman met a pirate and talk turned to their adventures on the sea. The seaman noted that the pirate had a peg leg, a hook, and an eye patch. The seaman asked, "So, how did you end up with the peg leg?"

The pirate replied, "We were in a storm at sea, and I was swept overboard into a school of sharks. Just as my men were pulling me out, a shark bit my leg off."

"Wow!" said the seaman. "What about your hook?"

"We were boarding an enemy ship and were battling the other sailors with swords," replied the pirate. "One of the enemy cut my hand off."

"Incredible!" remarked the seaman. "How did you get the eye patch?"

"A seagull dropping fell into my eye," said the pirate.

"You lost your eye to a seagull dropping?" the sailor asked incredulously.

"Well . . . ," explained the pirate, ". . . it was my first day with the hook."

Sir Francis Drake

1

Sir Francis Drake

Pirate or Hero?

Hero or villain? Could the first Englishman to sail around the globe, a man knighted by Queen Elizabeth I for his daring deeds, and a man England considers one of its greatest heroes, truly be called a pirate?

Francis Drake began his life as the son of a poor Protestant preacher. Francis was born around 1540 in Devon, England, and lived on a farm. After finishing his chores, young Francis would escape to the salty sea, teaching himself to sail.

By 1563 the young man had learned enough to sail as third officer on a vessel in a fleet of six ships led by his cousin, John Hawkins. Together, they made several voyages to the Caribbean, where they sold smuggled goods to the Spanish colonies.

On one trip, in 1567, the cousins learned a hard lesson. While negotiating what seemed to be a friendly trade, their ships were suddenly under attack. Drake and Hawkins had no way of knowing that the king of Spain had forbidden his governors to continue trading with the smugglers. The king had given orders to attack all English vessels.[1]

Four of the ships were destroyed, and the two men were lucky to survive the battle. Both their ships barely made it back to England with crews suffering from thirst and starvation. Drake never forgot the betrayal, and from then on he devoted his life to revenge on Spain.

Four years later Drake plotted his retaliation. The queen of England commissioned him as a privateer. This gave him permission to rob and plunder ships or towns flying flags of her enemy, King Philip II of Spain. Upon his return from a voyage, Drake would be expected to hand over all goods seized during his expeditions, such as China silks, linens, and fine dishes, as well as gold and silver coins. He would then be offered a percentage of the treasure as payment for his efforts.

In the tropical jungle surrounding Spanish colonies along the Caribbean, escaped African slaves shared Drake's hatred for the Spanish. They helped Drake lead many battles against the towns. The Spanish quickly learned to fear his anger, although

Sir Francis Drake, an English commissioned privateer, attacked Spanish ships, seized their valuable possessions, and returned the riches to England. The city of Cartagena (shown here), now in Columbia, was captured by Sir Francis Drake in 1586.

Drake stood a mere five feet five inches tall.[2] They called him El Draque (The Dragon).

One battle was to be the greatest of them all. Drake planned to rob the king's treasure house in Nombre de Dios (present-day Nicaragua). Twice a year, Spanish treasure ships would arrive at this busy port to load the gold and silver mined in the faraway mountains. The gold and silver were brought to the treasure house by mule train.

In July 1572, Drake anchored his ships. Then his men paddled canoes in the dark of night toward the sleepy town. They marched in, beating drums and sounding trumpets to make their group seem larger. Unfortunately for Drake, not everything went as planned. Many townspeople panicked. A group of Spanish soldiers opened fire, hitting Drake in the thigh. A thunderstorm broke out, leaving Drake's men with useless weapons. Their guns couldn't shoot wet gunpowder, and their bows couldn't fire arrows from wet bowstrings.

His men were ready to give up, but not Drake. Even as blood poured from his leg, he announced to his men, "I have brought you to the treasure house of the world."[3] He forced the doors open, but the house was empty. They were too late. The treasure fleet had already sailed. The next mule train shipment would not arrive for several months.

Drake and his men escaped and sailed north to where they could remain hidden, recuperate from their wounds, and wait. By late fall the treasure fleet had arrived in Nombre de Dios, so Drake knew the mule train carrying silver from the mountains of Peru was on its way.

Instead of trying another attack in town, Drake and his men ambushed the mule train on the trail. The surprised Spanish soldiers were forced to retreat from the musket fire. Drake found the mules loaded with bars of silver—more treasure than he and his men could carry. They took what they could, then buried the rest to be dug up later.

Francis Drake returned triumphant to England in 1573 a very rich man. The queen of England was so pleased that she commissioned him to ferry soldiers to places in Ireland to help put down a rebellion. During the long sailing trips, Drake enjoyed the comfort of fine furniture in his cabin and dining on silver dishes. Musicians accompanied the journeys, playing trumpets and viols. During prayer services, Drake knelt on a cushion and recited psalms, then the musicians played an accompaniment to hymns.[4]

In December 1577, Queen Elizabeth sent Drake on a secret expedition against the Spanish colonies in the New World (America). At the time, Drake didn't realize his fleet of five ships and 166 men were beginning the first trip around the world.

The fleet set sail from Plymouth, England, and crossed the Atlantic Ocean. Two of the ships were lost or abandoned. The remaining three ships, including Drake's newly named *Golden Hind*, passed through the Strait of Magellan into the Pacific Ocean. There they met terrible storms. For months the ships were unable to find clear weather and were often treacherously close to the coastline. One of the ships went down, and a second turned back for England, only to arrive in disgrace. The *Golden Hind* was left to journey alone.

Drake sailed north, always flying the English flag, often raiding Spanish settlements and plundering

Spanish ships. Drake and his men took what they wished, such as stores of food, and most important, maps of this new area unfamiliar to the English sailors.

Still, Drake was not cruel to his victims. Francis Pretty, one of Drake's gentlemen-at-arms, wrote that after one ship "yielded unto us [a] good store of wine," they sent the crew away, "giving them a butt [large cask] of wine and some victuals [food], and their wearing clothes."[5]

One of the ships Drake hoped to find was the *Nuestra Señora de la Concepcion,* a ship nicknamed *Cacafuego.* It was rumored to be laden with treasure. When a lookout spied the ship, Drake tried a tactic often used by pirates. He disguised his ship as being slow and harmless by towing mattresses and heavy pots.[6]

He then used his own invented tactic—the broadside. When the Spanish ship came astern, Drake presented a line of heavily armed men along one side of the *Golden Hind,* while trumpets sounded. The bombardment of both cannon and musket fire would have shattered the enemy's hull, rigging, and sails. The treasure ship had no choice but to surrender. It took days to transfer the immense treasure of gold, silver, coins, pearls, and precious stones to the *Golden Hind.*

Francis Pretty wrote: "Our General [is now] sufficiently satisfied and revenged; and supposing that her Majesty at his return would rest contented with this service."[7] Not only did Drake finally feel revenged, but he also knew King Philip II would be outraged and would send Spanish authorities after him. Drake quickly ended his looting.

By June of 1579, Drake had reached a position far up the northwest coast, probably near where the states of Washington, Oregon, and California are now. He traded with natives who offered "feathers and bags of tabacco for presents."[8] Drake dropped anchor in a harbor, now believed to be the San Francisco Bay area, naming it Nova Albion. Finally, he headed west into the Pacific, loaded with treasure. Drake reached Plymouth, England, in September of 1580, becoming the first commander to sail around the world.

The queen received many complaints from the Spanish ambassador about "this vile *corsair*," demanding justice.[9] She ignored the ambassador. Instead of punishing Drake as a pirate, she treated him as a hero, knighting Drake on the deck of the *Golden Hind*.

Sixteen years later, Sir Francis Drake began his last expedition, again with his cousin John Hawkins. While in the West Indies, the two became sick and died, as did many of their men. In a farewell to the national hero, the remaining crew set fire to the fort at Portobelo and several vessels. Amid a roll of muffled drums, they sent out a cannon salute.[10]

Sir Henry Morgan

2

Sir Henry Morgan
Morgan the Terrible

During the 1600s, settlers had moved in on the Spanish hold over the Caribbean. First came the English, then the French, the Dutch, and even runaway slaves and criminals deported from their homeland. Most of these settlers cultivated farms of tobacco, sugar, and cotton. Others, however, formed gangs who hunted wild cattle that roamed the islands. The men would cut their meat into long strips and smoke it over a slow fire into *boucan*, giving them the name *boucaniers*, or buccaneers.

These unruly men were a nuisance to Spanish colonies and thought of as criminals. However, many English in Jamaica felt the presence of buccaneers protected their island from a Spanish attack. In 1662 the governor, Lord Windsor, had become worried about the threat of a Spanish attack. He formed a squadron of these unruly men to attack first. The buccaneers chased Spanish ships and plundered their coastal towns.

One of the officers heading these raids was Henry Morgan. Like Francis Drake, Morgan was an English privateer, operating under a commission that defended his fierce actions against the Spanish. But there the similarities ended. While the English consider Drake a hero, Morgan's bold terrorist activities eventually brought accusations of piracy—even by those in his homeland.

In 1635, Henry Morgan was born in Wales to a rich farmer. Not much is known about his childhood, except that he preferred fishing to studying. He later admitted he had "left school too young" and had been "more used to the pike than the book."[1]

By the time Morgan was twenty-eight, he had sailed in the West Indies, cut cane on sugar plantations, and settled in Jamaica. There, he joined the regiment ordered to raid Spanish settlements.

Henry Morgan must have impressed the buccaneers during these attacks. Two years later he was able to recruit a loyal crew. With the help of Indian guides, the men covered lakes, swamps, and mud, both on foot and in small boats, through the tropical jungle. They surprised sleepy towns, ransomed prisoners, and made off with all the valuables they could carry.

Their return to Jamaica in 1665 caused quite a stir. Peace had been signed with Spain, and the privateer's commission had been canceled. Luckily for Morgan, the new governor, Sir Thomas Modyford, felt the privateers were necessary for Jamaica's protection. He defended their actions.[2]

During this time, Morgan married his cousin Mary Elizabeth. She was a woman well respected among island society. But by January 1668 the informal group of buccaneers in the Caribbean, calling themselves Brethren of the Coast, looked at her husband as their chief—leader of the pirates.[3]

The thieves operated under their own honor code of conduct and established rules of operation. Before a raid, each pirate knew there would be no pay. Instead, the loot taken would be added together and then divided among them.

Morgan's next assignment was to find out if the enemy had plans to invade Jamaica.[4] At this point, Morgan's actions appeared more like those of a pirate than of a patriotic privateer. True, he was under the cover of a government commission. But instead of using a small crew to question enemy prisoners, he assembled seven hundred men and set his sights for Puerto Principe, Cuba. The town had never before been attacked, so it would have plenty of valuables to plunder.

Morgan was unaware that the mayor of Puerto Principe had been warned in advance. Men hid along the trail, armed with axes and muskets. They surprised the buccaneers. Still, after an exhausting four hours of battle, the pirates took over the town. Morgan threatened that the townspeople would see their homes "in a flame . . . wives and children torn in pieces before your faces."[5]

When the Spaniards surrendered, the pirates locked everyone in the churches. Then the pirates went to neighboring towns, demanding ransom for the release of prisoners. Morgan's demand? Five hundred cows and enough salt to preserve the meat. The ransom was delivered to where his ships were anchored, and the prisoners were forced to do the butchering on the beach.[6]

Though there is no physical description of Henry Morgan, one of his Dutch buccaneers, Exquemelin, later wrote of Morgan's spirited energy and talent of persuasion: "[Morgan] always communicated vigour with his words, infused such spirits into his men . . . they all resolved to follow him."[7] Proof of this talent is that Morgan convinced his 460 men to next target the treasure port of Portobello, along the coast of Panama.

On June 26, 1668, the pirates silently paddled canoes to the coast. They marched forward on foot with muskets, cutlasses, shot pouches, and grenades. They soon took over the town, a fortress, and headed next for Santiago Castle. Morgan dragged old men, young girls, and religious people from the churches. They were used as human shields for the advancing

Sir Henry Morgan used the valuables he seized from ships for his own personal use while commissioned as a privateer.

buccaneers and forced to carry ladders to the castle walls.

The pirates tortured prisoners so they would reveal places of hidden wealth. "Many of them died upon the rack, or presently after," wrote Exquemelin.[8] Morgan sent a note to the Spanish governor of Panama City, threatening to burn the town. He received 250,000 pesos worth of silver and gold as ransom. All the while, Morgan flew the English flag, even though England was now at peace with Spain.

In 1669, Morgan gathered more buccaneers on the heavily armed warship HMS *Oxford*. When they came upon a French vessel, he extended a phony invitation to the officers for a dinner on his ship, but quickly put them in irons below deck. The buccaneers celebrated their easy takeover by drinking and shooting pistols and cannons into the air. Suddenly, whether by a careless accident or sabotage, the stored gunpowder blew up! The *Oxford* was blown to smithereens. Of the hundreds of men on board, fewer than thirty survived. One survivor was Captain Morgan.

Perhaps Morgan felt lucky. His next bold move was to take over a French pirate's ship, renaming her *Satisfaction*. He then headed for Maracaibo, Venezuela, with his small fleet. After navigating the narrow straits into the lagoon, Morgan found the town almost deserted. He savagely tortured the few people there, stretching their legs with ropes until their joints cracked. He burned fingers and toes until the sufferer finally shrieked where his savings were hidden.[9] From there, Morgan took his men to the nearby village of Gibraltar to do the same.

Meanwhile, the Spanish had positioned three flagships at the mouth of the lagoon, blocking Morgan's only way out. Morgan was given a generous offer. The buccaneers would be allowed to escape if they left the stolen loot behind. When Morgan told this to his men, they shouted that "they had rather fight, and spill the very last drop of blood they had in their veins than surrender so easily."[10]

Fight, they did—a sneaky fight. The men first blackened logs to look like iron and arranged them on a captured Cuban ship to resemble a gun deck They next made wooden frames and clothed them, complete with caps on their stuffed heads, to look like a warship's crew. Finally, tar and brimstone were poured throughout, with a powder keg and fuse transforming the ship into a secret bomb.

Morgan sent this ship with a small crew on the pretense of new terms. As they approached the Spanish, Morgan's crew lit the fuse. Then the men escaped over the side of the ship and swam to the safety of another. By the time the Spanish realized the hoax, it was too late. The ship exploded, taking one of the Spanish ships with her. The men on the second Spanish ship panicked. While trying to escape the shooting flames, they ran aground and sank in the shallow water. The third Spanish ship was quickly taken over by the jubilant buccaneers.[11]

In the summer of 1670, an official letter from England ordered the buccaneers to stop plundering the Spanish. Morgan ignored the order and planned his largest raid. He recruited nearly every buccaneer in the Caribbean to target the rich city of Panama.

It would not be an easy raid. Sandbars forced the men to travel on foot. They marched through swamps and dense jungles infested with mosquitoes and dangerous snakes. They followed along the Cheques River under the hot tropical sun. Practically starving, they resorted to eating grass and leaves. They even boiled their leather bags until they were soft, then ate them. Finally, they came across a barn filled with maize and a field of livestock. They feasted themselves and regained enough strength to sack Panama.

The men attacked the Spaniards with no mercy, but they came away with small spoils to split. The city went up in flames, leaving nothing but a cathedral's stone tower and portions of other stone buildings.

In 1672, King Charles of England summoned Morgan to London to answer for his misdeeds. Morgan arrived on the HMS *Welcome,* a sick man. The trip in confined conditions on the cold North Atlantic had made him weak. Though he was under arrest, he was not imprisoned but was free to enjoy his time in England with friends, mounting his defense.

Many English still believed his raids against the Spanish were justified. In fact, by 1674 the peace between England and Spain had once again been broken. Instead of being imprisoned, Morgan was knighted by the king. It was the atrocities against innocent people, however, that left Morgan with a less than heroic reputation.

Morgan returned to Jamaica as its lieutenant governor. He owned plantations there where he grew sugar, cocoa, indigo, cotton and ginger, tobacco and grapes. Suddenly, Morgan turned against the buccaneers. He had always carried letters of marque, and he insisted that buccaneers who operated without such licenses should be executed. After ordering three pirates to a death by hanging, he explained in a letter to England: "One of the condemned is proved a bloody and Notorious villain and fitt to make an exemple of."[12]

In his early fifties, Morgan lived on his estate, drinking rum most of the day. He had developed a cough and swollen legs. On August 25, 1688, Sir Henry Morgan died. In his will, he left most possessions to Mary Elizabeth, his "very well and entirely beloved wife."[13] A funeral procession moved slowly through the hot, dusty streets of Port Royal as the ships in the harbor fired guns in a governor's salute.

Henry Avery

3

Henry Avery
The Arch-Pirate

For months the privateers on the ship *Charles II* waited to set sail, but their captain kept calling for delays. Without the opportunity to plunder, the men received no pay. They grumbled about their captain, who was said to be "addicted to Punch" and spent much of his time drinking.[1]

One man, first officer Henry Avery, paid attention to the grumbling and planned a mutiny. He was about to turn pirate. In fact, Henry Avery was to become the lucky pirate who found the instant success other pirates had only dreamed about.

English-born Henry Avery was of average height but rather fat. His fair complexion tended to burn a bright red in the sun. He wore plain clothes: a tricorn hat, breeches under a long waistcoat, and buckled shoes.[2] Hidden underneath this common appearance, however, was a smart man with a strong personality. Avery was able to convince the group of English and French men on the *Charles II* to show loyalty to one another over their country, and act on his plan of mutiny.

On May 7, 1694, Avery and his men took over the ship from their drunken captain and put him ashore. Avery renamed the ship *Fancy* and declared himself captain. "I am bound to Madagascar, with the design of making my own fortune," he announced.[3] He ran up the English flag along with his own, bearing four silver chevrons on a red field.[4]

Avery and his crew sailed south along the African coast. They plundered any ships they came upon, whether English, Danish, or French. They took provisions and arms, gold dust, brandy, and chests filled with linens and silks.[5] Before reaching Madagascar, Avery stopped at Johanna Island to work on the *Fancy* and make her a swift ship. He ordered the crew to scrape her hull to help her slide through the water faster. They removed deck cabins and hatches to give her more speed.[6]

As if attempting to protect himself from the crimes he was about to commit, Avery composed a letter to "All English Commanders." He advised them to fly their country's flag on their ships. "[I shall] never molest you," he wrote. He then added: "My men are hungry, stout, and resolute, and should they exceed my desire I cannot help myself."[7] Avery felt he shouldn't be held accountable for the actions of his men.

Soon, Avery sailed the *Fancy* to the Red Sea where he met other pirate ships. He convinced them to join him in a partnership. They planned to seize the merchant ships in the area, which were laden with spices and cloth or gold and coffee. In August 1695 they learned that treasure ships owned by the Mogul Empire in India were about to leave their port in the Red Sea. Avery knew these ships held many riches for their return to India. He would seize this opportunity of a lifetime.

The largest of the ships was the *Ganj-i-Sawai*. She was filled with silver and gold pieces. The ship carried six hundred passengers, many of them servants and members of the court of the emperor, the Great Mogul. When Avery spotted the *Ganj-i-Sawai*, he ignored the fact that the *Fancy* was both outgunned and outmanned. He ran up a pirate's "bloody flag" of solid red. Then he raced the *Fancy* to overtake the large, lumbering ship.

One of Avery's first shots crashed into the main-mast and damaged the rigging. It made the Great Mogul's ship impossible to control. The pirates quickly scrambled aboard with cutlasses and pistols, fighting ferociously against the soldiers. The battle lasted two long hours.

Finally, as screams of the dying faded away and gunpowder smoke disappeared, the soldiers surrendered. Avery and his pirate crew now possessed the *Ganj-i-Sawai*. In its great hold there were many slaves, attendants, rich jewels, gold, and silver. A saddle set with rubies, meant to be a gift for the Great Mogul, was now theirs.

The grand prize didn't come without a price, however. Many of the pirates were dead, too. The surviving pirates took revenge on their prisoners. Men were stripped and their possessions taken. Some were accused of hiding valuables and were tortured to reveal where they were hidden. Women were raped unless they threw themselves overboard or stabbed themselves with daggers, choosing death over the savage treatment of the pirates.[8] Through it all, Avery remained aboard the *Fancy*, not taking part in such cruelty.

When the tremendous loot had finally been divided among the crew, the ships scattered. Knowing he would be arrested and hanged if he ever returned to England, Avery sailed across the Atlantic to the Bahamas. He bribed Governor Trott with pieces of gold, elephants' ivory tusks, and other valuable items in exchange for protection in the Bahama Islands.[9] Now a rich man, Avery retired from his brief but infamous career as a pirate.

Of course, the Great Mogul was furious. He threatened to send his "mighty Army with Fire and Sword."[10] He wanted to rid all the settlements on the Indian coast of English people. The British East India Company, a large trading company, promised to search out Avery.

Henry Avery retired and disappeared from his life of piracy after he reached his financial goals. Rumors surrounding his misdeeds and disappearance made his name infamous. Here he is shown receiving a treasure chest on board a ship.

The news of Avery's battle with the *Ganj-i-Sawai* traveled to England, along with many rumors about his escape. Some said Avery captured and married one of the Great Mogul's beautiful daughters. Others said he offered the king of England money to pay off the national debt in exchange for a pardon for his crime.

In truth, Avery was tired of life as a fugitive and planned a secret return to Britain. In June 1696, Avery sailed a small sloop to Ireland under an alias, changing his name to Bridgeman. Though he was able to disappear and escape punishment, some of his men were not as lucky.

At one port an officer reported a small group of men who arrived with as many as thirty-two bags and so much money they could hardly carry it. Adding to their suspicion, the men foolishly spent that money without care. They "offered any Rates for Horses—Ten pounds for [an inferior Irish horse] not worth Forty shillings."[11]

In another port it was reported that passengers had pieces of muslin to trade—a material then made only in India.[12] These careless crewmen were captured, brought to trial in London, and were convicted. Eighteen were sent to America as convict laborers and six were hanged at Execution Dock.

One villain's last words were that the "inhuman treatment and merciless tortures inflicted on the poor Indians and their women still afflicted his soul." But another wasn't so repentant. He kicked off his shoes before being hanged, proving "those to be liars who had said he would die with his boots on."[13]

Of the intelligent commander, Henry Avery, no one knows. Some say the lucky pirate lived out his days in luxury on a tropical island. Others say merchants had swindled him of his riches, forcing Avery to end his days in poverty, "not being worth as much as would buy him a coffin."[14]

4

Samuel Bellamy
Pirate Prince

In 1999 treasure hunter Barry Clifford pulled off his diver's mask and grinned. He held out two silver coins—Spanish pieces of eight that had been blackened from centuries beneath the salty sea. "The last time a human touched them, they were either being handled by a pirate," Clifford said, "or being used to buy human lives."[1]

After fifteen years of searching for the ship, loot was finally pulled from the first pirate ship ever discovered in North America, the *Whydah Galley*. It had been a slave ship that was chased down by a band of pirates led by Samuel "Black Sam" Bellamy.

A young Samuel would have reveled in the discovery. Centuries earlier he, too, had been a treasure

Samuel Bellamy—nicknamed "Pirate Prince"—was proud of the
Whydah ship—one of his largest captures. It is shown here in the
storm that destroyed it in 1717.

hunter. When in his early twenties, Samuel Bellamy left his home in England. He and his friend Paul Williams hoped to find their fortune among sunken Spanish treasure ships along the coast of Florida. All they found, however, was a mosquito-infested area swarming with other men hoping to salvage from the same wrecks.

The young men soon signed on with a band of buccaneers under the command of pirate captain Benjamin Hornigold. Captain Hornigold was loyal to his homeland and held to a policy of not plundering English ships. Many of the buccaneers disagreed with this policy. In the spring of 1716, Hornigold left the group and sailed off with twenty-six loyal followers.

Young Bellamy remained on the *Mary Anne*, and the crew quickly elected him their new captain. He and Williams sailed to the Virgin Islands with ninety men. They found a small islet perfect for use as a base during the winter months. They cleaned their ships in the bay. On shore they formed a settlement of shacks made of driftwood and shelters of palm fronds.

Once settled, the men set to piracy. One day they took several small fishing boats and a French ship, plundered their goods, then returned the vessels to their owners. The next day they chased down two more ships. This time, after taking some provisions, they kept one vessel, the *Sultana*. They persuaded some of the men aboard the *Sultana* to "go on account," meaning to sign on as a pirate.

Samuel Bellamy, like most pirates, flew a menacing flag similar to the one shown here to intimidate those who were under attack.

The following day they took a merchant ship, which had sailed from Ireland and was laden with ham, butter, and cheese. After "having taken out what provisions they wanted and two or three of the Crew, [the pirates] let her goe."[2] It is said that Bellamy and his crew took more than fifty ships that winter of 1717.

As he pursued his prey, Bellamy must have made a striking figure on deck in his long velvet coat and his shoes with silver buckles. Though it was fashionable at the time to wear a powdered wig, he wore his dark hair long and tied back with a satin bow. A sword was slung over one hip, and he carried pistols in his sash.

Bellamy's wasn't the only group of pirates in the area. Other bands had based themselves in and around the Caribbean, including another pirate with a frightening reputation—Blackbeard. The Royal Navy ship, HMS *Scarborough*, was sent to the Caribbean to rid the area of pirates. Though it was still the wintry month of February, Bellamy decided the area was no longer safe. It was time for him to leave.

As the buccaneers cruised the Windward Passage near Cuba aboard the *Mary Anne* and the *Sultana,* Bellamy spied a large merchant ship. The *Whydah* had sailed from London to Africa to pick up slaves and ivory. It then headed across the Atlantic to Jamaica. While in the Caribbean, most of the slaves had been traded for other goods. The eighteen-gun ship was now laden with sugar, indigo, silver, and gold, ready to sail home to England. Bellamy decided the ship would never reach her destination. He was right.

For three days Bellamy chased the fast ship. He managed to take it "without any other resistance than [its captain] firing two chase guns at the Sloop [before coming] to an anchor."[3] This is probably because most pirates showed mercy to those who surrendered without a fight.[4]

Bellamy was one of those pirates. He immediately exchanged ships, claiming the *Whydah* as his own. Then he released its captain and crew and allowed them to escape aboard the *Sultana*. He transferred guns to his new flagship, making it strong enough to overcome any merchant ship of the time.

By early April 1717, the *Whydah* headed up the eastern coast of the New World. Spring often brings bad weather to the northeast, and one night the pirates met a violent storm. Lightning flashes and roaring winds penetrated the dark night. After a loud thunderclap, Bellamy swore to the gods that he was "sorry he could not run out his Guns to return the Salute."[5]

A week later the crew reached the shores of Virginia, where they easily took many vessels. Their plunder wasn't always silver and gold, but was often bales of silk or cotton, barrels of tobacco, carpenter's tools, or spare sails.[6] A ship from Bermuda might provide rum, sugar, or molasses.

Bellamy's large crew was a mixture of many nationalities. Though most were from England and Ireland, some were colonials, Indians, or former slaves. Blacks on captured slave ships would be offered a choice to either join up with the pirates or continue to the New World for a life of slavery.[7] Aboard the *Whydah*, the men were no longer considered of different heritage. *Pirate* became their one nationality, and they were loyal only to the Brethren of the Coast.

Bellamy captured a ship that had been commanded by a Captain Beer. The pirates plundered what they could, then sank the ship. Before marooning the men on Block Island off the coast of Rhode Island,

Bellamy spoke of his disgust with what he considered an unjust society. "They rob the poor under the cover of Law," he said. "We plunder the rich under the protection of our own courage."[8] He asked who among the men would choose to join his buccaneers. Captain Beer declared it would mean breaking the laws of God and man. Bellamy yelled, "I am a free prince [with] authority to make war on the whole world . . . this my conscience tells me."[9]

On April 26, 1717, it was with this clear conscience that Samuel Bellamy met his match—a nor'easter. The storm howled through the thick fog. The hard rain with gusty winds of seventy miles per hour made waves reaching thirty feet high. The *Whydah* struck a sandbar. A giant wave rolled her over. Cannons fell from their mounts. Amid pirate screams, the beautiful ship was torn apart, spilling her contents into the sea.

The next morning bodies littered the beach. Only two men survived—John Julien, an Indian, who escaped, and Thomas Davis, a carpenter, who was captured and put on trial in Boston for his crimes as a pirate.

Samuel Bellamy, the pirate prince, and 144 of his men had met their watery grave, leaving behind artifacts for treasure hunters of the future.

Edward Teach

Edward Teach

Blackbeard

He was a frightening man, large and strong. He had a long, bushy beard and barked bold orders in a booming voice. In only a few short years of piracy, Edward Teach became one of the most famous pirates—Blackbeard.

Teach hadn't always answered to this famed name. About thirty years before, around 1680, he was born in Bristol, England.[1] Teach was probably raised in a respectable family, because he was an educated man, able to read and write. As a young boy, he may have read books that told of surprising discoveries around the world and the excitement of a life at sea.

Throughout Teach's boyhood, England was at war, first fighting against France and later battling

Spain. It is believed that Edward Teach had been a privateer, one of the men who attacked and plundered ships flying the flags of England's enemies. When the war ended, rather than choosing to earn an honest living, he joined the crew of the pirate captain Benjamin Hornigold. By now there were an estimated two thousand rough, unruly men on the high seas who "appeared more like thieves and less like potential allies."[2]

Many pirates were based in the Bahamas where they could find women, alcohol, and eager ears to tell of daring sea adventures. Among the blue-green waters of the tropical islands, stories of Teach's fearsome reputation spread. Once, after entering a tavern and demanding a drink, Teach mixed gunpowder in his rum, set it on fire, then guzzled the explosive mixture![3]

In the spring of 1717 both Benjamin Hornigold and Edward Teach captained sloops and sailed from the Bahamas to the coast of colonial America. On their way, if they spotted a lone ship they boldly ran black flags up their masts and went after the victim. Surrounding the vessel from both sides, they fired as they closed in. These two men captured many ships, taking their barrels of flour, wine, or whatever cargo pleased them.

Sometimes, the ships themselves became the prize. One prize was a French ship, the *Concorde*, which Teach renamed *Queen Anne's Revenge*. He armed it with forty guns and a crew of nearly three hundred men. Soon after, Hornigold retired from piracy, though the captain would later boast that he was "the one to discover and train the great Blackbeard."[4] Teach tested his new ship and crew by overtaking large ships, stealing what they wanted, and then burning what was left.

Teach had quite a frightening appearance. Though beards were not common in those days, Teach grew his very long. It was black and covered much of his face, almost to his eyes. He would twist it into tails and tie them with ribbons. During battles, he wore a sling over his shoulders with pistols hanging in holsters across his chest. He often lit hemp cords that had been soaked in saltpeter to burn slowly and stuck them under his hat.[5]

One day at sea, Blackbeard said to his comrades, "Come, let us make a hell of our own and try how long we can bear it." They went down into the ship's hold, closed up the hatches, filled pots full of brimstone, and set them on fire until they were almost suffocated. All except Blackbeard cried out for air. Finally, Blackbeard opened the hatches, pleased that he had held out the longest.[6] "Damn ye, ye yellow———!" he snarled. "I'm a better man than all ye milksops put together!"[7] It is no wonder that this fierce and wild-looking man with smoke billowing around his face was rumored to be the devil himself.

Like many pirates, Blackbeard spent winters in the Caribbean, then headed north during the summer months. When Blackbeard returned to America, he immediately went to Governor Eden of

Blackbeard and his crew spent summer months off the eastern U. S. coast. Here, his crew is partying on the coast of North Carolina.

North Carolina. Blackbeard surrendered under a proclamation of King George I of England. It pardoned all pirates who took an oath never to engage in piracy again. After this pardon, Blackbeard was free to market his goods.

Though most English colonies had closed their ports to pirates, North Carolina allowed them to market their plunder. One place the pirates looked to steal more treasures was Charleston, South Carolina. It was the busiest port in the southern colonies. The pirates would then travel north and sell the stolen goods at reasonable prices.

In May 1718, Blackbeard used his overpowering fleet to set up a blockade outside Charleston. For a week Blackbeard captured all ships heading in or out of the harbor. He held their crews and passengers hostage. Blackbeard did not ask for money. Instead, he demanded medical supplies as a ransom. When the chest of medicines finally arrived, he looted the ships, then set the captives free.

Humiliated by Blackbeard's blockade, Governor Johnson of South Carolina reported the uselessness of the king's pardon. "Some few [pirates] indeed surrender and . . . and then several of them return to the sport again."[8] Blackbeard now had in his hold the richest booty of his life, and the anger of an entire city.

Blackbeard was very familiar with the ever-changing North Carolina coast. He knew of the inlets between sandbars that were excellent hideouts for a pirate ship that needed to anchor for repairs. Yet, Blackbeard grounded the *Queen Anne's Revenge* on one of these sandbars.

In November 1996 a team of underwater archaeologists found what they believe to be the wreck of the three-hundred-ton ship. Among the finds was a pewter syringe, which could have been from the medicine chest that had been the ransom payment for the Charleston hostages.[9]

Many historians believe the grounding of the *Queen Anne's Revenge* was no accident. It was but a scheme to get away with most of the loot, her sails, tackle, and provisions. Together, Blackbeard and his friend Israel Hands went into a small sloop, leaving the large, disabled ship behind. Seventeen men were marooned on an island "where there was neither Bird, Beast or Herb for their Subsistance."[10] Luckily for them, they were rescued two days later.

Blackbeard once again presented himself to Governor Eden for a pardon. The governor knew that Blackbeard had not changed his ways but merely wanted "a more favourable opportunity to play the game again."[11] Eden was powerless against the notorious pirate.

Though Blackbeard settled in town for a while, he soon returned to the sea. At times, Blackbeard had trouble controlling his unruly crew. An entry in his journal reads: "Such a Day—Rum all out:—Our Company somewhat sober: Rogues a plotting;—great Talk of Separation:—So I look'd Sharp for a Prize." After the capture of a merchant ship, the mood appears to have changed. "Such a Day took one, with a great deal of Liquor on board . . . then all Things went well again."[12]

Access to rum was not the only way Blackbeard kept his men in line. One night he shot Israel Hands through the knee, crippling him. His explanation was that if "he did not now and then kill one of them, they would forget who he was."[13]

The people of the Carolinas did not forget. Blackbeard's pillaging of so many ships disrupted the trade business. Since Governor Eden could not control the pirates, the merchants of North Carolina sent a plea for help from the north. Governor Spotswood of Virginia offered a generous one hundred pounds reward for the capture of Blackbeard.[14]

Lieutenant Maynard of the Royal Navy was chosen for the mission. Sixty men in two sloops searched with Maynard through the channels and shoals, avoiding treacherous shallow areas. One evening they spotted Blackbeard's ship, *Adventure,* near Ocracoke Island, North Carolina, separated from them by sandbanks.

Blackbeard must have seen his attackers, yet he spent the evening drinking with friends. His voice boomed across the still waters of the night. He was asked where he had buried his money in case anything happened to him in the upcoming battle. Blackbeard responded that "no Body but himself, and the Devil, knew where it was, and the longest Liver should take all."[15]

In the first gray light, the battle began. Blackbeard bellowed for his attackers to identify themselves. They responded, "You may see by our Colours we are no Pyrates."[16] He then fired his guns, hitting one sloop broadside and eliminating it from the rest of the battle.

Maynard was able to steer his ship alongside Blackbeard's, and the two crews swirled into close fighting combat. Cutlasses clanged and guns fired. Grenades exploded. Blackbeard was slashed across the throat and shot in the chest, yet the strong man continued charging his enemies. Over and over,

Blackbeard was stabbed and shot, until this great man of terror finally fell.

Lieutenant Maynard ordered the bearded head cut off and hung from the bowsprit of his sloop. This trophy of his victory over the famous pirate was taken back to Virginia and displayed on a pole.

A legend tells of the headless corpse being tossed into the water, then swimming three times around the sloop as if searching for its missing head. It was "the end of that courageous brute, who might have passed in the world for a hero had he been employed in a good cause."[17]

6

Anne Bonny and Mary Read

Pirate Queens

In the early 1700s, thousands of pirates swarmed the Bahamas. Their small fast sloops terrorized merchants who had to maneuver large slow ships around the islands. Imagine, then, the terror of the crew on a French ship, laden with valuable silks and satins, as they spot a woman standing at the bow of an approaching sloop. She repeatedly strikes a human figure with a grappling hook that drips with blood. The horrified crew surrenders without a fight. Later on, they discover that the woman had soaked a stuffed puppet, the hook, and a sail in turtle's blood in order to stage the horrible show.[1]

Anne Bonny and Mary Read

The woman who shared Blackbeard's passion for theatrical displays was Anne Bonny. She was the most famous of women pirates.

The red-haired beauty was born in Ireland, the illegitimate daughter of a married man and his servant maid. Her father, attorney William Cormac, was fond of his young daughter, but because the townspeople knew of his affair, he chose to disguise her as a boy. The pretense was that the young relative was in training to become a lawyer's clerk.

The ruse was discovered, and due to the scandal, his wife left him and he lost many clients. Cormac then took the servant, Peg Brennan, and daughter, Anne, to Charleston, South Carolina, to start a new life as a family. There, he became a successful merchant and settled on a large plantation.

Anne was a young spitfire, rumored to have once stabbed a serving girl with a knife during a fit of rage. She was thought to have stopped a would-be rapist by beating him ferociously.[2] Around 1716 the teen disappointed her father by marrying a poor sailor, James Bonny, and sailing with him to New Providence. The marriage was soon over, for three years later Anne Bonny met the dashing pirate Jack Rackham and fell in love. Rackham was known around the islands as "Calico Jack" for the calico-cotton pants he wore.

He returned Anne's affections, giving her jewelry from his booty. He offered to buy her from her husband—a common form of divorce at the time.[3] Married women were considered their husband's property, but James Bonny refused the offer to sell his wife. Instead, he complained to Governor Woodes Rogers of the Bahamas to uphold the law in his favor. The governor ordered Anne's return to her husband. He threatened to have her whipped, the usual punishment for an adulteress. Under cover of men's clothing, Anne escaped to the sea with her lover.

The adventurers, Jack Rackham, Anne Bonny, and fellow pirate Pierre Vane, set about plundering small ships around Jamaica. They focused mainly on local merchants and small fishing boats. One ship they set their sights on was owned by John Haman. Bonny flirted with the owner on the pretense of having some business with him. She boarded the ship to ask questions and look around. Her true purpose was to see how many hands were on deck and what kind of watch they kept.[4]

Using the information she learned, the pirates chose a dark, rainy night to paddle their canoe silently to the ship. Bonny climbed aboard, dressed as a seaman, and armed with sword and pistol. She went straight to the cabin and threatened the two men there that if they "make a Noise, she would blow out their Brains."[5] After sending the two men to shore, the pirates made off with the sturdy ship and claimed it as their own. They were now ready to strengthen their company and plunder even more.

For six months the pirates plundered small prizes. One day they captured a Dutch merchant ship. After taking what provisions they wanted, Rackham recruited new sailors from the crew. One new recruit had blue eyes and light hair. Rackham noticed Bonny spent a lot of time with this new sailor and became very jealous. Finally, Bonny revealed why she had formed such a close friendship—the new recruit was another woman, Mary Read, dressed as a man!

Like Anne, Mary Read had been born illegitimate. Her mother had married a sailor who went to sea and never returned. After discovering that she was pregnant with another man's child, she took her infant son to the English countryside to hide the scandal. Mary's young brother died just before she was born. Her mother then disguised Mary as the dead brother and raised her daughter as a boy.

As a young teen, Mary was a serving boy and later joined the army. Eventually, she fell in love with another soldier.[6] She revealed her secret, and the two married. They opened a tavern called The Three Horse Shoes. Mary Read's happiness was short-lived, for her husband was suddenly struck with a mysterious fever and died.

Once again, she donned men's clothing. She hired on as crew to the Dutch ship that had been heading for the West Indies until its attack by Rackham's pirate crew. Though King Charles I of England had decreed that "no woman shall falsify her sex by wearing a man's clothing," poor, unmarried women did not have many options in the world at that time.[7] Often, disguising themselves as men was the only alternative to a life of prostitution.

Anne Bonny dressed in men's clothes to escape her husband and begin a life of piracy. Mary Read later joined her on the ship, also disguised as a man. After the boat and crew were captured, both Bonny and Read revealed they were pregnant, received leniency for their condition and escaped execution.

That summer of 1720, Rackham, Bonny, and Read kept the secret. This was not only daring for the women, but it was brave of Rackham as well. According to pirate code, no man was to allow a disguised woman aboard a pirate ship at sea, under penalty of death.[8]

The three concealed the truth, fighting side by side in many battles. The two women fought as fiercely as the men, cursing and using weapons with skill. Even though they kept up their rough image, the other pirates on board may have discovered their secret. Still, the women were allowed to remain on the ship. Bonny was described as being a good leader and Read as having excellent navigational skills.[9]

Eventually, Read became smitten with Tom Deane, one of the sailors on board. He had been forced to join the pirate crew. During a quarrel with another pirate, Deane was challenged to a duel. Read was afraid for her lover's life because he wasn't a skilled fighter. However, she didn't want him branded a coward.[10] Her solution was to provoke an argument with the pirate as well. Duels had to be scheduled for a time when they would be on land. It was against pirate code to fight one another while on board.[11]

Read scheduled a time to set ashore for her own fight, two hours earlier than when the pirate was to fight her lover. As in a formal duel, they stood back-to-back. They counted paces apart, then fired their pistols. Both were left standing, so they switched to cutlasses. The baited pirate never made it to his second duel.

By late summer 1720, Governor Rogers had completed a fortress in Nassau's harbor. He had many soldiers to defend the area from both the Spanish and the pirates. Because it was no longer an area of easy prey, most pirates left the Bahamas for Jamaica. Of course, this didn't please the governor of Jamaica at all. In October he commissioned Captain

Jonathan Barnet of the ship *Tyger* to rid his area of pirates as well.

It didn't take long before Captain Barnet discovered Calico Jack's ship anchored in a sheltered cove. Dry Harbor Bay was a hidden spot where pirates felt safe to rest and party. When Barnet arrived on the scene, Rackham and his men were too drunk to put up much of a fight. Many hid in the ship's cargo area.

As incoming fire whistled over their heads and cut a path through the rigging, Anne Bonny and Mary Read stood their ground on deck. They fired their pistols and slashed their cutlasses. Read screamed for the men to come out and help fight, but they remained below deck. She fired her pistol at them in anger, killing one of the cowardly pirates before the ship's surrender.[12]

The pirates were brought to trial in November 1720, where they faced numerous charges. They were said to have attacked fishing boats to steal their fish and tackle. They had fired at and taken merchant sloops and put fear into the hearts of area sailors.[13]

One witness was Dorothy Thomas, who had been the victim of one of the crew's earlier attacks. She testified that the two women "wore men's jackets, and long trousers, and handkerchiefs tied about their heads." The reason she knew they were women was "by the largeness of their breasts."[14]

All the pirates were found guilty and sentenced to death by hanging. Bonny and Read escaped the noose because they were both pregnant, and the law protected the unborn. Soon after the trial, however, Read was seized with a violent fever and died.

It is thought that Bonny returned to her father in South Carolina. Before she left, she visited Rackham but left him little comfort. She told him that "if he had fought like a Man, he need not have been hang'd like a Dog."[15] As he climbed the scaffold, it marked not only the end of Calico Jack Rackham, but the end of an era—the Golden Age of Piracy.

Bartholomew Roberts found "pleasure and ease" in piracy.

7

Bartholomew Roberts
Black Bart, the Crimson Pirate

In November 1719, Bartholomew Roberts was the second mate aboard the *Princess*, a slave-trading ship on its way to Africa. His heart must have raced as men on an approaching ship ran up a black flag, identifying themselves as pirates. Roberts was captured, along with many of the *Princess*'s crew. He was forced to serve pirate Captain Howell Davis aboard the *Royal Rover*.

During the next few weeks, Roberts quickly discovered that "in an honest Service there [are] . . . low Wages, and hard Labour; in [piracy] . . . Pleasure and Ease . . ."[1]

Bartholomew Roberts was born in Wales around 1682 and, like many young sailors, began an honest career by joining the merchant navy. The years at sea had given him excellent navigational skills and the ability to make bold decisions. This must have impressed the pirates aboard the *Royal Rover*. When Captain Davis was killed in an ambush during a shore raid, Roberts was elected the pirate captain's replacement.

Before reaching his fortieth birthday, the dark-complexioned Roberts, nicknamed Black Bart, had not only joined the pirates but had become their leader. "A merry Life and a short one, shall be my Motto," he declared.[2]

The crew may have found their new captain a bit odd, for he was very particular about his clothing and insisted on drinking only tea.[3] It would take a daring man to criticize the stern Captain Roberts. He was a man of discipline, even over unruly pirates.

He wrote a pirate's code of conduct, a set of articles that each man aboard ship had to sign. Some of the articles spelled out what each pirate was entitled to have. Article I stated that every man had a vote. Article X said officers were due one and a quarter share of any plunder. Other articles specified how the crew was expected to act. Article III prohibited gambling, and Article IV demanded lights out at eight o'clock.[4]

During a trip to the West Indies, Roberts came upon a large fleet of forty-two ships bound for Portugal. The pirates easily captured one of the ships, then chased after another. They fired a broadside, disabling the prize ship. The booty was tobacco, sugar, and gold, along with fancy trinkets that included a cross set with diamonds meant for the king of Portugal.[5]

Satisfied with their loot, the pirates hid out on Devil's Island, French Guiana. Roberts bribed the governor with the jeweled cross, in exchange for their safety.[6] The men remained on the island for weeks, spending their loot on women, rum, and gambling. Meanwhile, Roberts was on the lookout for his next plundering opportunity. He heard of a ship due to arrive from Rhode Island, laden with provisions. Roberts gathered forty men and a small sloop to go after the ship. The *Royal Rover* was left behind under the command of his lieutenant, Walter Kennedy.

The pirates searched for a week, but never found the Rhode Island ship. The disappointed men, short on supplies, returned to Devil's Island. To their surprise, Kennedy had disappeared with the *Royal Rover*, along with the rest of the crew and all of their treasure!

In January 1720, Roberts came up against ships commissioned by the governors of Barbados and Martinique to stop piracy in the area. In the battle many of Roberts's men were killed or wounded. A cannon shot a big hole in the pirate ship, but Roberts and his men managed to escape. He was so angry at the attempts on his life that he designed a new pirate flag. On it, a figure of himself stood upon two skulls—those of the governors who had ordered his capture.[7]

By June the pirates had recovered from their wounds and were ready to plunder again. They sailed to Newfoundland with their black flag hoisted high. Musicians beat drums and blared trumpets while the pirates seized, looted, then burned and sank the ships of their victims. In all, they captured twenty-two ships at anchor. Roberts claimed one ship of twenty-six guns as his own, renaming her *Royal Fortune*.

Roberts sailed with about one hundred men across the Atlantic to the African coast. There, he took many prizes in his well-armed vessel. On July 13, 1720, Roberts took the *Samuel*, commanded by Captain Carry. After boarding the ship, the pirates stripped all passengers and crew of both their money and clothing, then threatened to shoot anyone who did not give up their valuables.

Next, they used axes and cutlasses to tear into trunks and boxes, shooting pistols into keyholes of chests to force them open. If they found goods they didn't want, "instead of tossing them into the Hould again they threw them over-board into the Sea."[8] They cursed their victims and threatened that if anyone dared try to stop them, they would "put fire with one of their Pistols to their Powder, and go all merrily to Hell together!"[9]

When the pirates discovered a supply of fine wines, they didn't wait to use corkscrews. Instead, they slashed off the bottle necks with cutlasses and drank from the broken bottles.[10] They set Captain

Carry free to sail off when they spied another ship. Then they did the same all over again.

Though Roberts was not a drinking man, most of his crew enjoyed their rum punch. A ship full of drunk, wild men could not have been easy to control. Once, when Roberts was insulted by a crewman, Roberts killed the man on the spot. The man's friend cursed Roberts and struck him, but the friend's revenge was short. He was tied to the mast and endured two lashes from each officer as punishment for his actions against the captain.[11]

Meanwhile, across the Atlantic in Virginia, six pirates had faced a trial and execution. The famous Blackbeard had been slaughtered. When Roberts heard of the killings, he vowed his revenge against the Virginia authorities. Governor Spotswood panicked. He had heard that when Roberts captured a French ship, the French captain was hanged. Some of those aboard were tied to the mast and shot or had their ears sliced off.

Afraid of Roberts's vengeance, Spotswood ordered armed batteries to guard the mouths of rivers. He also sent letters to governors up and down the coast to ask them for help.[12] He wrote: ". . . what inhuman Treatment must I expect . . . who have been markt as the principal Object of their Vengeance, for . . . making so many of their Fraternity to swing in the open air of Virginia."[13]

Roberts never did get his revenge. In the summer of 1721, he captured a merchant ship, the *Onslow*, took it as his own, and again gave his ship the name *Royal Fortune*. One passenger was a clergyman. The pirates asked him to remain on board, promising him a share of their loot in return for his making punch and saying prayers for them. He refused the offer, so they set him free, taking nothing from him but "three Prayer-Books and a bottle screw."[14]

Roberts now commanded four vessels and about five hundred men. The pirates cruised up and down the African coast, capturing and plundering as they went. One day they took a ship with fine sausages on board. The pirates strung the meats around their necks, making fun of the unfamiliar food, then threw them overboard.[15]

Another day they took over a fleet of slave ships. Roberts allowed the captains of the vessels to buy back their ships and cargo for a ransom. One of the captains refused, so the ship was set afire. The poor slaves who were shackled together in pairs had a miserable choice—burn to death in the flames or jump into shark-infested waters to drown and be eaten.[16]

By now, Roberts had heard that two Royal Navy ships were patrolling the African coast. Most of the HMS *Weymouth*'s crew were so sick with malaria that it was forced to anchor. Captain Ogle of the HMS *Swallow* kept searching for the notorious pirate. Although there were no radios or telephones for communication, and there were unlimited coves for ships to hide in along the coasts, news of where pirates operated managed to travel from ship to ship.

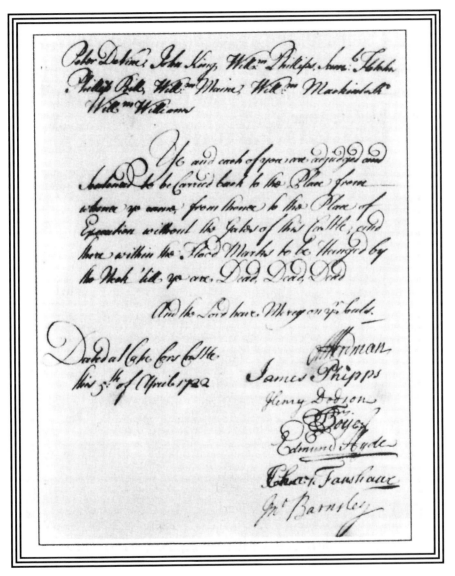

Roberts was captured by pirates and forced to work. After he discovered the riches that were there for the taking, he decided to become a pirate. Above is a death sentence passed against nineteen members of Roberts' crew in 1722.

It took months of searching, but Captain Ogle finally heard from a fisherman that Black Bart was in the area.

On February 10, 1722, Roberts watched the warship approach the *Royal Fortune*. The tall dark man was dressed in his finery: a crimson waistcoat and breeches, a hat complete with a red feather, and gold jewelry around his neck. He had tied two pistols together by a silk sling and had positioned them over his shoulder.

Roberts ordered the black flag raised and prepared for battle. The *Swallow* came near and fired. Grapeshot, a cluster of iron balls, tore open the Crimson Pirate's throat and sent him staggering over the blocks of a gun. One of his men ran over and, when he discovered his captain was dead, he cried openly.[17] The pirates threw Roberts overboard, complete with his jewelry and weapons, honoring his own request.

Of the surviving pirates, seventeen were sentenced to prison. Fifty-two were hanged at Execution Dock at the low-water mark, and remained there for three tides. Some of the bodies were dipped in tar to preserve them and left hanging where all approaching ships would see them.

Before his hanging, one of the convicted pirates prayed desperately for forgiveness. Another exclaimed, "Heaven? . . . Give me Hell, it's a merrier Place: I'll give Roberts a Salute of 13 Guns at Entrance."[18]

8

John Paul Jones
Father of the American Navy

"I have not yet begun to fight!" are the famous words of American hero John Paul Jones. Some even honor him with the title "Father of the American Navy." To the British, however, he was a thieving pirate.

The famous name John Paul Jones wasn't the one young John was given at birth. He was born July 6, 1747, to John and Jean Paul, on an estate in Scotland where his father was the gardener. Even as a young boy, John Paul knew he wanted to be more than a gardener or farmer. Instead, he imagined a life at sea.

Whenever he could, John played war games with friends, standing on a cliff and yelling commands to imaginary ships at battle. He went to the nearby port of Carsethorn to climb aboard ships and talk to the

John Paul Jones

sailors. In smoke-filled rooms he listened to the rough, bearded men talk about their adventures in icy seas or along warm tropical shores.

When he turned thirteen, John signed on as an apprentice to a merchant, studying navigation, French, and poetry. He worked aboard the ship *Friendship* as a cabin boy. The ship headed first to Barbados for rum and sugar, then on to colonial Virginia for tobacco.

John made many trips back and forth across the Atlantic. Whenever he was in Virginia, John stayed with his older brother, William, who worked as a tailor in Fredericksburg. John later wrote about the colonies, saying the area was "my favorite country from the age of thirteen when I first saw it."[1]

In April 1767, John Paul worked aboard *Two Friends*, a small slave-trading ship. At the time, slave trading was considered a reputable business, but John soon discovered its cruelty on the ship. He hated seeing the harsh treatment of the seventy-seven Africans crammed below deck. He resolved to get out of the abominable trade as quickly as he could.[2]

When he was in Jamaica he met one of the owners of a merchant ship on its way back to Scotland. Jones took the opportunity for a trip home. During the voyage, both the owner and first mate died of yellow fever. Since John Paul was the only person aboard who knew how to navigate, he took over command. "A warrior is always ready," he later said.[3] The other owners were so impressed with the twenty-year-old who brought their ship home safely, they offered him command of the merchant vessel.

John Paul was a small, thin man, about five feet five inches in height. He enjoyed reading the good literature of his day, including Shakespeare. As a captain, John was difficult to work under. Many men complained of his quick temper. During the ship's second voyage under his command, John felt his carpenter, Mungo Maxwell, was lazy. He ordered Maxwell tied to the rigging to be whipped. The punishment left several striped scars across Maxwell's back. After the ship put ashore in Tobago, Maxwell lodged a complaint against John Paul, but the judge dismissed the charges.

When Maxwell sailed home aboard another ship, John Paul may have thought that would be the end of his troubles with the carpenter. Unfortunately, Maxwell took ill during the voyage home and died at sea. Maxwell's wealthy father accused John Paul of beating his son so badly that his son died as a result of his injuries.

A trial resulted. John Paul wrote his mother that his accusers had been afraid to confront him, and that there was no foundation for the trial that lasted six long months.[4] Though John Paul was eventually cleared of the murder charge, he would forever live with that rumor.

By late 1773, John Paul was in command of a larger merchant ship, *Betsy*, with an established trade operating in the West Indies. Again, it was the second voyage that affected his fate. John Paul was now twenty-six years old, a talented navigator and a crafty trader. However, when he announced his plan to invest in more cargo and would hold his men's wages until they reached their home port, mutiny brewed.

The angry crew's ringleader towered over the small captain. Suddenly, the furious man lunged forward. He was ready to bludgeon John Paul for refusing to pay the crew's wages. John Paul quickly drew his sword and ran him through, killing the rebellious mutineer immediately. This time there was no doubt that John Paul was directly responsible for a man's death. What a court would have decided is unknown. The man known as Captain Paul disappeared.

In 1774 a John Paul Jones appeared in Virginia. Why he changed his name has been debated. Some say the Jones surname was chosen because it was so common it couldn't be easily traced. Others say John Paul was impressed with two friends, brothers Allen and Wylie Jones. It is said that he told them he would "take the name of Jones and make it famous."[5]

When Jones traveled to Philadelphia, he befriended Benjamin Franklin and Joseph Hewes. They were convinced the American colonies needed a navy. The navy's beginning was small—a four-ship fleet of armed merchant ships. But by then, the American Revolution had begun. On December 7, 1775, John Paul Jones was commissioned first lieutenant on the U.S.S. *Alfred* of the Continental navy. He was the first to hoist the flag of freedom for display across the ocean.

John Paul Jones is often called the "Father of the American Navy" due to his effort against the British during the Revolutionary war. Above is the first battleship ever owned by the United States of America, the U.S.S. *Alfred.* It was commanded by John Paul Jones.

The English viewed American soldiers as pesky rebels, and they considered American sailors nothing but pirates. Who else were crazy enough to attempt war at sea against Great Britain? The English Parliament passed a law allowing their soldiers to treat all Americans captured at sea as "traitors, pirates and felons."[6] The Americans, of course, proclaimed them heroes.

In March 1776, Jones proved his skill in a battle against the HMS *Glasgow* off the shores of Rhode Island. Jones was then named a Continental captain, drawing thirty-two dollars a month as salary from

Congress. He commanded the sloop *Providence* on a cruise with orders to seize, sink, burn, or destroy that of enemies.[7] For two years Jones wreaked havoc on Britain. Wearing the naval uniform of a blue coat with red lapels, he led raids, "destroying the fisheries and burning all of the vessels that I could not carry away."[8]

In 1778, Jones sailed near Scotland's shores in the *Ranger*, now considered an enemy of his birthplace. He sank a Scots schooner, then a Dublin sloop. He boarded an anchored ship and set it afire. His attacks were sudden and made during the secrecy of night.

To Jones, it was his patriotic duty. He once expressed his patriotism in a letter, stating: "I was indeed born in Britain; but I do not inherit the degenerate spirit of that fallen nation, which I at once lament and despise." Instead, he felt a bond with Americans who, "reward the man who draws his sword only in support of the dignity of freedom."[9]

On April 23, 1778, Jones sent men ashore near his boyhood home, to Lord Selkirk's mansion. He planned to kidnap Selkirk and hold him hostage to use in trade for Americans held by the enemy. Unfortunately for Jones, Selkirk was away from home. Jones's men took silver plates as their booty. Lady Selkirk later described Captain John Paul Jones as "a great villain as ever was born, guilty of many crimes and several murders."[10]

When back at sea, the *Ranger* met the British man-of-war HMS *Drake* in a ship-to-ship battle. On April 24, 1778, Jones managed to capture the ship, even though the *Drake* had more arms and almost double the manpower. In only twenty-eight days, Jones had performed a land raid, taken and destroyed many merchant ships and captured the warship HMS *Drake*. With every ship Jones took, however, his fearsome reputation grew in England. He was called a traitor and a pirate.

On September 23, 1779, Jones fought his most famous battle aboard the *Bonhomme Richard* against the British ship *Serapis*. The battle raged through the night, with the two ships so close to each other that cannons were useless. Both vessels were in flames. Even as sparks flew from the rigging and the water rose around his sinking ship, Jones did not give up. When asked for his surrender, Jones refused, saying, "I have not yet begun to fight!" Jones's men finally overpowered the English soldiers. Victory again belonged to John Paul Jones. ——

Once the English discovered their coasts had been attacked and their warships fallen, they looked at the American rebels differently. They realized it was possible their large navy couldn't protect all of their coasts. The people began asking for peace with the colonies. Soon the war was over.

Many years later, Jones suffered from jaundice, swelling of his legs, and pneumonia. On July 20, 1792, at forty-five years old, John Paul Jones died in Paris, France. In 1905 his body was brought to the Naval Academy Chapel in Annapolis, Maryland, and now rests in a memorial tomb.

9

Jean Laffite
Gentleman Smuggler

The nineteenth century English poet Lord Byron wrote of Jean Laffite: "He left a corsair's name to other times, Linked one virtue to a thousand crimes."[1]

The same man remembered for his heroic role in the Battle of New Orleans during the War of 1812, had long been known as "The Terror of the Gulf" for his years of piracy in the Gulf of Mexico. Though United States presidents have both condemned and excused his actions, Jean Laffite thought of himself as a privateer, acting on behalf of the country that needed him.

Three brothers, Alexandre, Pierre, and Jean Laffite were born in Port-au-Prince, Haiti. Their

Jean Laffite meets with General Jackson and Governor Claiborne.

French father and Spanish mother had fled Spain to escape the Inquisition. During the Inquisition, the Spanish executed thousands of people who didn't share Roman Catholic beliefs. Their mother died soon after Jean was born, so their Jewish grandmother raised the boys. She hated Spain, and taught her grandsons to feel the same.[2]

Alexandre Laffite became a privateer, known to the enemies of France as Dominique You. The short, stocky man with dark hair and dark eyes was an expert cannoneer, taking aim at Spanish ships. Powder burns left scars on his face, which made him look fierce. While Pierre and Jean waited for the day when they could join their brother as privateers, they became inseparable friends. They attended private school, then went on to military training where they learned to use dueling weapons with skill.[3]

One would find it hard to guess that Dominique and Jean were brothers, for Jean was tall, slim, and handsome. He often washed his hair with potash and gunpowder to make his hair and mustache a reddish color. The color complimented his hazel eyes, meticulous dress, and refined manners.[4]

In 1806, Jean Laffite arrived in the area that is now the southwest corner of Louisiana. While the boundary between Spanish Texas and the United States was being fought over, this corner of marshy lowlands was known as the Neutral Strip. It was left unoccupied by troops of either nation. Laffite took this island's fishermen and roguish seamen and organized them into a crew of buccaneers and smugglers. This home of alligators, panthers, and bears was soon swarming with slave traders and pirates.

Laffite opened a blacksmith shop as a cover for his smuggling. He sold goods captured by privateers well trained as cannoneers and deckhands. The men would come across a prize ship, remove its cargo, then sink or destroy the vessel. They took over Spanish ships loaded with gold, silver, and jewels from Mexico. They attacked merchant ships laden with cloths, spices, and furniture. Laffite then sold the goods at discount prices.

When the United States outlawed the importing of slaves in 1808, Laffite found smuggling slaves a new way to make money. He hired more men to unload goods and to man warehouses used to store captured slaves until they could be sold.

By 1809, Pierre and Jean Laffite controlled a large ring of thieves—as many as five thousand men. They brought in such a huge amount of goods that Laffite needed to build a new warehouse every month![5] Merchants from all over the Mississippi Valley bought stolen goods from Laffite. Cotton plantation owners and sugar planters traveled for days to reach Laffite's warehouses to buy smuggled slaves.

Everyone in the area knew of the handsome, powerful Jean Laffite. It is said that a French aristocrat who escaped the guillotine contacted Laffite to help him settle in Louisiana. The aristocrat was frightened when he saw Laffite's rough men swarm into dugouts, paddle to the warship, and begin boarding. Laffite calmed him by explaining, "These are my friends and will do my slightest bidding."[6]

In 1812, the year Louisiana became a state and war was declared against Great Britain, Laffite held an auction to sell a large amount of goods all in one day. He chose a spot halfway between his warehouses in Grande Terre and the city of New Orleans called The Temple. It was a large mound of shells the Indians had built long before. The auction was a great success.

So great was its success that other area businesses suffered. Merchants complained to Governor William Claiborne. He sent for the United States Army to help prevent smuggling in the area. One night the army troops discovered boats filled with smuggled goods. One boat tried to escape, but after a brief battle the men were taken prisoner. One of those prisoners was Jean Laffite. He had no trouble making bail, though, and he never showed up for trial.

Governor Claiborne called Laffite a bandit and posted a reward for Laffite's delivery to a sheriff. Two days later the citizens of New Orleans were treated to Laffite's humor. Laffite had posted his own handbill offering a much larger reward for Governor Claiborne's delivery to him.[7]

Claiborne and Laffite shared a dislike for each other. However, only one year later they found themselves fighting on the same side. Laffite received an anonymous report, dated August 8, 1814, that British troops had arrived on the coast of Florida in gunboats.

In September, British officers who wanted Laffite's help in attacking New Orleans approached him. They needed his knowledge of the area to guide them through the maze of wetlands. One of the captains reminded Laffite that the governor had declared him an outlaw, and that Jean's brother Pierre was in jail.

While holding off his answer to the British, Laffite sent his packet of information to Governor Claiborne, warning of the planned attack. "Though proscribed (condemned to death) by my adoptive country, I will never let slip an occasion of serving her," Laffite explained.[8]

Could the governor believe in Laffite's honor, or was it a trick to get him to release Pierre? One of Claiborne's advisers defended the Laffite brothers. "The United States is their adopted country. They see it threatened by an enemy they hate."[9]

Meanwhile, Pierre escaped from jail. Laffite wrote again, hoping the governor would understand where his honor lay. "I am the stray sheep wishing to return to the flock," he wrote.[10] Claiborne may not have been convinced. However, General Andrew Jackson recognized that Laffite controlled the best sailors in the world and the most skillful gunners. Laffite could supply the army with ammunition and cannons. He could navigate through the familiar streams and lagoons with skill.

Laffite helped Jackson organize transportation through the marshland. They cut barges one hundred feet long from cypress trees and shuttled them back and forth, loaded with men and ammunition.[11]

During the Battle of New Orleans, on January 8, 1815, Laffite fought well. He helped keep New Orleans from enemy hands, and his followers helped General Jackson's forces win a victory. Later, U.S. President James Madison pardoned Laffite and his men for their acts of piracy.

It wasn't long before Laffite was back to his old pirate ways. By 1817, Laffite had established a new base for his privateers. The pirates captured Spanish slavers and brought the slaves to pens on Galveston Island. At times, the pens held a thousand or more African slaves. Buyers came from all over to purchase slaves at one dollar per pound.[12] Eventually, the base was ordered evacuated by the United States Navy in 1821.

It is believed that Laffite then changed his base of operations to Mexico. There, he continued his illegal activities until 1826, when he became mortally ill and died. This may not be true, however. A journal, supposedly written by Jean Laffite, was found in 1976. In it he tells of bribing a priest to report his death in order to escape the Spanish who wanted him for piracy. He then changed his name to Jean Lafflin and moved to South Carolina.

LAFITTE,

THE FAMOUS PIRATE OF THE GULF OF MEXICO.

Jean Laffite put a hold on his piracy to participate in the Battle of New Orleans under General Andrew Jackson. Shortly after he was pardoned by President James Madison, Lafitte and his crew returned to piracy.

Through the years, the legends of Jean Laffite have grown. One story is that in June 1815, Laffite loaded aboard his ship many chests that contained Emperor Napoléon's fortune. Napoléon had hoped to escape to Louisiana, but Laffite sailed away without him. Laffite's crew buried the immense treasure on the shores near New Orleans.

Years later, an ex-slave who had known Laffite described hunters in search of Laffite's buried treasure. "About three feet under the ground was an iron chest . . . with a whole lot of gold inside," he said. "Three men go into them woods . . . and never but two came out of there, and they brought the other horse to carry the gold!"[13]

Over the years, dying sailors left maps and directions to find the buried treasure. No one knows for sure that treasure is out there, but many still search. Once, a man stumbled on what he thought were a pile of bricks. When he took a brick home, he discovered it was silver bullion. He returned to the site, but never found the remaining bricks again. Legend says the ghost of Laffite himself guards his buried treasure.

Who knows which of the stories are true? Whether pirate, thief, or hero, Laffite is a man of many legends.

Cheng I Sao

10

Cheng I Sao
Dragon Lady

In the early 1800s, a vicious couple led thousands of pirates in plundering ships in the South China Sea. He was the daring Cheng I and she was his wife, the rebellious Cheng I Sao (wife of Cheng). When Cheng I drowned during a typhoon, the pirate captains quickly elected his widow as their chief. She accepted the honor and acted forcefully.

This was unusual, for in those days Chinese women were expected to follow Confucian standards. They acted as servants to their fathers, husbands, and sons. They tottered on feet that had been bound to keep them small and delicate. Cheng I Sao defied this authority. By 1810 this strong-willed woman led the most powerful band of murderous pirates in the area.

Lady Cheng was probably born aboard a pirate ship. Unlike most European pirates who felt women aboard a ship were bad luck, entire families ran piracy in China. Some lived their whole lives on junks, flat-bottomed ships with large sails, and never set foot on land. Women still served their fathers, and were usually responsible for rowing and handling the small crafts up and down the coasts. But women also took part in combat and sometimes commanded ships.[1]

The Cheng family had been involved in piracy since the 1600s. In 1801, Lady Cheng joined this large family by marrying Cheng I. She moved onto his ship and fought beside him in battles.

When they weren't plundering ships, the Chengs relaxed with other pirates. With ocean water lapping at the side of the ship, they played cards and smoked opium. The close quarters were often dirty and overrun with rats that were bred for food. Rice cooked with caterpillars was a common meal. As a prisoner later described, there is "hardly a living thing the pirates didn't eat."[2]

One day the Chengs captured a fisherman and his fifteen-year-old son, Chang Pao. Though captive children were usually sold into slavery, this particular boy pleased the Chengs, so they adopted him and raised him as their own.

In 1807, when Cheng I reportedly drowned during a November typhoon, his wife, Cheng I Sao, had no trouble assuming his leadership duties. First, she expanded the force until eight hundred large and one thousand small junks with seventy thousand men floated the seas up and down the coasts from Canton to Vietnam. Next, she divided them into six squadrons, each sailing under their own colored flag. Finally, she took the adopted son, Chang Pao, and put him in charge of the largest squadron, the "Red Flag Fleet."

Cheng I Sao and her band of pirates were merciless. They went after every ship they came across. While at sea, if they caught one of the emperor's ships they murdered everyone aboard. Merchants didn't suffer as harsh a fate, their ships were merely plundered. But if the sailors fought back in self-defense, they were met with death.[3] Prisoners were offered a choice to either join the band of pirates or suffer a death by flogging. Women and children were sold as slaves to be smuggled into Singapore, Bombay, or San Francisco.[4]

People who lived in villages along the shore weren't safe from the pirates either. The villagers had to pay to avoid raids. If they didn't pay, the pirates stormed into their homes, took prisoners, and cut off their heads. Some men tried defending their homes. They hid their women and children and prepared for battle. During one fight, shopkeepers climbed onto the rooftops and threw crocks of slippery sauce at the pirates. This act of self-defense angered the pirates. They set the bamboo barricade afire.[5]

Even while leading such terrorist acts, Cheng I
Sao enforced a code of conduct among the pirates. It
was similar to that established centuries earlier by
Bartholomew Roberts, although more rigid and with
more severe penalties. Pirates had to register all plunder, and they couldn't secretly take loot or they
would be severely whipped. If any crew member
dared to go ashore without permission, his ears
would be sliced. A second offense meant death.[6]
Pirates who broke the code of conduct were beaten
or viciously murdered.[7]

Before battles, Chang Pao might stand on the
bow of his ship, dressed in a purple silk robe and
black turban. Cheng I Sao would call Chang Pao to
consult with their guardian spirits. The two were
very religious and kept statues in a temple aboard
their flagship.[8] The pirates believed the gods protected Chang Pao and gave him superhuman
powers.[9] He often went ashore to visit priests in their
temples and give donations.

In 1808 the Chinese imperial government sent
fleets out to destroy Cheng I Sao and her empire.
The first fleet, led by Admiral Kwo Lang, reached her
ships in July. She was ready, hiding most of her ships
behind a headland while the rest met for battle.
During a fight that lasted sixteen hours, the hidden
ships came out to attack the soldiers from behind.
The pirate victory made Admiral Kwo Lang so
ashamed that he committed suicide.[10]

The second fleet approached Cheng I Sao, but her six hundred armed junks met the soldiers head on. General Lin Fa was afraid and he quickly ordered a retreat, but it was too late. The wind had died, so their sails were useless, and they could not escape. Pirates held daggers in their teeth and swam across to the enemy, swarmed aboard their ships, and killed the general and his crew.[11]

In November, Admiral Tz'uen Mao Szun's imperial ships managed to surround Cheng I Sao's fleet during the night. They sent a fire ship against the pirate's boats, which were anchored close together. One of Cheng I Sao's prisoners had kept a detailed log of his three-month captivity. In it he described the horrible sight of the fire ship's approach. "Her hold was filled with straw and wood . . . boxes of combustibles on her deck, which exploded alongside of us."[12] Some of the rigging on the pirate ships ignited in a flash of flames, forcing Cheng I Sao to withdraw. Just as the admiral relaxed, Cheng I Sao and her pirates turned around for a surprise attack. "Everyone fought to save their own skins," described a soldier, "and scarcely a hundred people survived."[13]

On January 29, 1810, the pirates beat gongs and shot firecrackers to celebrate the lunar New Year. But hidden by the merriment, a mutiny brewed. The chiefs of the six squadrons bickered with one another. The green squadron leader's jealousy of Chang Pao's easy rise to command grew so deep that it came to a battle.[14] After sinking sixteen of the red squadron's junks and killing three hundred men, the green leader went to the governor of Macau to apply for amnesty. It was granted.

Cheng I Sao decided it might be the right time to end her pirate ways, but she would negotiate for something in exchange. As if she were a royal queen, she presented herself to the governor amid music and gun salutes. The governor agreed to her tough demands. Each of her pirates received food, wine, and money along with a pardon.[15] Her devoted Chang Pao was named a lieutenant of the imperial army and allowed to keep about thirty of his junks.[16] The South China Sea was finally rid of the violent pirates.

Cheng I Sao married Chang Pao and, through the years, saw him rise in rank to colonel before he died in 1822. It is believed that she spent the rest of her life near Canton, running a gambling house or a smuggling operation until she died in 1844 at the age of sixty-nine.

Glossary

amnesty—To surrender in return for a certificate of pardon.

booty—Goods obtained illegally as a result of battle.

bowsprit—A heavy spar pointing forward from the vessel's front.

brigantine—A combat ship that could carry a crew of one hundred men and a large cargo.

broadside—Firing all guns from one side of a ship.

buccaneer—A term for hunters who smoked meat on the island of Hispaniola, later used to describe pirates and privateers.

corsair—Pirates or privateers who operated in the Mediterranean.

cutlass—A short, curved sword

doubloon—A former Spanish gold coin

fireship—A vessel loaded with explosives and used as a bomb by igniting it and directing it to drift among an enemy's warships.

galleon—A large ship of three or more masts used in combat.

gally—A low, flat boat propelled by oars.

gibbet—A wooden gallows from which criminals were hung for public view as a warning to pirates.

jolly roger—A pirate flag with skull and crossbones.

junk—Chinese flat bottomed ship with large sails and a high stern.

letter of marque—letter of employment in the capture of enemy merchant shipping and to commit other hostile acts otherwise be condemned as piracy.

man-o-war—A warship.

merchant ship—A cargo ship involved in commerce.

privateer—One with a certificate from government that authorizes any attack or seizure of vessels of a hostile nation.

schooner—A ship with two masts for great speed and a shallow hull that allowed navigation in shallow waters.

sloop—A shallow, single-masted vessel with a long bowsprit, favored by pirates because of its easy handling.

strike colors—Lower ship's flag as sign of surrender.

Chapter Notes

Preface
1. Alvin Ung, "Pirates Becoming Increasingly Violent," *Pocono Record*, March 16, 1999, p. C8.

Chapter 1. Sir Francis Drake
1. David Cordingly, *Under the Black Flag: The Romance and the Reality of Life Among the Pirates* (New York: Random House, 1995), p. 38.

2. Simon Winchester, "Sir Francis Drake Is Still Capable of Kicking Up a Fuss," *Smithsonian Magazine*, January 1997, <http://www.smithsonianmag.si.edu/smithsonian/issues97/jan97/drake.html> (April 2002).

3. Cordingly, p. 27.

4. George Malcolm Thomson, *Sir Francis Drake* (New York: William Morrow, 1972), p. 136.

5. Modern History Sourcebook: "Francis Pretty: Sir Francis Drake's Famous Voyage Round the World, 1580," from C.W. Ellot, Voyages and Travels: Ancient and Modern, with Introductions, Notes, and Illustrations, The Harvard Classics, ed. vol. XXXIII (New York: P.F. Collier and Son, 1910), <www.fordham.edu/halsall/mod/1580Pretty-drake.html> (March 5, 2002).

6. Cordingly, p. 30.

7. Pretty, <www.fordham.edu/halsall/mod/1580Pretty-drake.html> (April 4, 2002).

8. Ibid.

9. Cordingly, p. 31.

10. William Wood, *Elizabethan Sea Dogs* (New Haven: Yale University Press, 1918), p. 229.

Chapter 2. Sir Henry Morgan

1. David Cordingly, *Under the Black Flag: The Romance and the Reality of Life Among the Pirates* (New York: Random House, 1995), p. 44.

2. John Ure, *The Quest for Captain Morgan* (Great Britain: Constable & Company Ltd., 1983), pp. 81–82.

3. Alexander Winston, *No Man Knows My Grave* (Boston: Houghton Mifflin, 1969), p. 48.

4. Ibid., p. 50.

5. Ibid., p. 51.

6. Ure, p. 101.

7. A. O. Exquemelin, *The History of the Bucaniers of America* (London: William Whitwood, 1695), p. 48.

8. Ibid., p. 52.

9. Ibid., p. 61.

10. Ibid., p. 70.

11. Ure, p. 141.

12. J. Franklin Jameson, "Sir Henry Morgan to Sir Leoline Jenkins, March 8, 1682," *Privateering and Piracy* (New York: The Macmillan Co., 1923), p. 134.

13. Winston, p. 48.

Chapter 3. Henry Avery

1. Captain Charles Johnson [Daniel Defoe], *A General History of the Robberies and Murders of the Most Notorious Pyrates*, Reprinted (New York: Carroll & Graf, 1999), p. 35.

2. Frank Sherry, *Raiders and Rebels* (New York: Hearst Marine Books, 1986), p. 68.

3. David Cordingly, *Under the Black Flag: The Romance and the Reality of Life Among the Pirates* (New York: Random House, 1995), p. 21.

4. Sherry, p. 72.

5. J. Franklin Jameson, "Examination of John Dann, August 3, 1696," *Privateering and Piracy in the Colonial Period* (New York: The Macmillan Co., 1923), pp. 165–166.

6. Sherry, p. 73.

7. Ibid., p. 74.

8. Ibid., p. 78.

9. Jameson, pp. 169–170.

10. Johnson [Defoe], p. 38.

11. J. Franklin Jameson, "Abstract, Letters from Ireland, June 16–July 7, 1696," *Privateering and Piracy in the Colonial Period* (New York: The Macmillan Co., 1923), p. 161.

12. Ibid., p. 163.

13. Sherry, p. 83.

14. Cordingly, p. 23.

Chapter 4. Samuel Bellamy

1. Donovan Webster, "Pirates of the *Whydah*," *National Geographic,* May 1999 <www.nationalgeographic.org/whydah/story.html> (March 6, 2002).

2. J. Franklin Jameson, "Examination of John Brown, May 6, 1717," *Privateering and Piracy in the Colonial Period* (New York: The Macmillan Co., 1923), p. 294.

3. Ibid., p. 295.

4. David Cordingly, *Under the Black Flag: The Romance and the Reality of Life Among the Pirates* (New York: Random House, 1995), p. 129.

5. Captain Charles Johnson, *A General History of the Robberies and Murders of the Most Notorious Pirates,* (London: Ch. Rivington, 1724), p. 586.

6. William J. Broad, "Archeologists Revise Portrait of Buccaneers as Monsters," *The New York Times,* March 11, 1997, Section C, page 1.

7. Webster <www.nationalgeographic.org/whydah/story.html> (March 6, 2002).

8. Donald G. Shomette, *Pirates on the Chesapeake* (Centreville, Md.: Tidewater Publishers, 1985), p. 185.

9. Ibid.

Chapter 5. Edward Teach

1. Philip Gosse, *The Pirate's Who's Who* (Boston: Charles E. Lauriat Co., 1924), p. 291.

2. Kris E. Lane, *Pillaging the Empire: Piracy in the Americas, 1500–1750* (Armonk, N.Y.: M. E. Sharpe, 1967), p. 171.

3. Robert E. Lee, *Blackbeard the Pirate: A Reappraisal of His Life and Times* (Winston-Salem, N.C.: John F. Blair, 1974), p. 19.

4. Ibid.

5. Captain Charles Johnson [Daniel Defoe], *A General History of the Robberies and Murders of the Most Notorious Pyrates* Reprinted (New York: Carroll & Graf, 1999), p. 70.

6. Lee, p. 23.

7. Norman C. Pendered, *Blackbeard, the Fiercest Pirate of All* (Manteo, N.C.:Times Printing Co., 1975) <www.ocracoke-nc.com/blackbeard/tales/blcknc05.htm> (March 6, 2002).

8. David Cordingly, *Under the Black Flag: The Romance and the Reality of Life Among the Pirates* (New York: Random House, 1995), p. 206.

9. Pete Taylor, "Have They Found Blackbeard's Smoking Cannon?" *Aqua Magazine,* February/March 1999 <http://www.aquamag.com/aqua/fm99flots.html>(May 1999).

10. Johnson [Defoe], p. 59.

11. Donald G. Shomette, *Pirates on the Chesapeake* (Centreville, Md.: Tidewater Publishers, 1985), p. 199.

12. Frank Sherry, *Raiders and Rebels: The Golden Age of Piracy* (New York: Hearst Marine Books, 1986), p. 243.

13. Shomette, p. 203.

14. Johnson [Defoe], p. 62.

15. Sherry, p. 248.

16. Johnson [Defoe], p. 65.

17. Ibid., p. 67.

Chapter 6. Anne Bonny and Mary Read

1. Ulrike Klausmann, Marion Meinzerin, and Gabriel Kuhn, *Women Pirates and the Politics of the Jolly Roger* (New York: Black Rose Books, 1997), p. 192.

2. Frank Sherry, *Raiders and Rebels: The Golden Age of Piracy* (New York: Hearst Marine Books, 1986), pp. 266–267.

3. Ibid., p. 267.

4. Captain Charles Johnson, *A General History of the Robberies and Murders of the Most Notorious Pyrates*, (London: Ch. Rivington, 1724), pp. 624–625.

5. Ibid., p. 625.

6. David Cordingly, *Under the Black Flag: The Romance and the Reality of Life Among the Pirates* (New York: Random House, 1995), p. 61.

7. Klausman, Meinzerin, and Kuhn, pp. 204–205.

8. Cordingly, p. 69.

9. Klausman, Meinzerin, and Kuhn, p. 207.

10. Captain Charles Johnson [Daniel Defoe], *A General History of the Robberies and Murders of the Most Notorious Pyrates* Reprinted (New York: Carroll & Graf, 1999), p. 136.

11. Klausmann, Meinzerin, and Kuhn, p. 207.

12. Sherry, p. 276.

13. Cordingly, p. 63.

14. Ibid., p. 64.

15. Johnson [Defoe], p. 144.

Chapter 7. Bartholomew Roberts

1. Captain Charles Johnson [Daniel Defoe], *A General History of the Robberies and Murders of the Most Notorious Pyrates*, Reprinted (New York: Carroll & Graf, 1999), p. 230.
2. Ibid.
3. Alexander Winston, *No Man Knows My Grave* (Boston: Houghton Mifflin, 1969), p. 36.
4. Johnson [Defoe], p. 195.
5. Ibid., p. 190.
6. Donald G. Shomette, *Pirates on the Chesapeake* (Centreville, Md.: Tidewater Publishers, 1985), p. 218.
7. Johnson [Defoe], p. 219.
8. J. Franklin Jameson, "Extract from the Boston News-Letter, August 22, 1720," *Privateering and Piracy* (New York: The Macmillan Co., 1923), p. 314.
9. Ibid., p. 315.
10. Ibid., p. 316.
11. Johnson [Defoe], pp. 210–211.
12. Shomette, p. 229.
13. Ibid.
14. Johnson [Defoe], p. 215.
15. Ibid., p. 218.
16. Ibid., p. 221.
17. Johnson [Defoe], p. 230.
18. Ibid., p. 233.

Chapter 8. John Paul Jones

1. Lincoln Lorenz, *John Paul Jones: Fighter for Freedom and Glory* (Annapolis, Md.: United States Naval Institute, 1943), p. 11.
2. John S. C. Abbott, *Life of John Paul Jones* (New York: Dodd, Mead and Company, 1874), p. 12.
3. Lorenz, p. 17.
4. Abbott, p. 15.

5. Mary Jones Polk Branch, *Memoirs of a Southern Woman "Within the Lines,"* and a Geneological Record, (University of North Carolina at Chapel Hill, 1998), pp. 88–99. <http://docsouth.unc.edu/branch/branch.html (April 2002).

6. Gerard W. Gawalt, *John Paul Jones' Memoir of the American Revolution* (Washington, D.C.:Library of Congress, 1979), p. 15.

7. Samuel Eliot Morison, *John Paul Jones: A Sailor's Biography* (Boston: Little, Brown and Company, 1959), p. 60.

8. Gawalt, p. 8.

9. Abbott, p. 20.

10. Lorenz, p. 157.

Chapter 9. Jean Laffite

1. Mel Leavitt, "Great Characters of New Orleans" (The New Orleans Tourism Marketing Corporation, 1999) <http://www.neworleansonline.com/gcno-lafitte.htm> (May 1999).

2. Jane Lucas de Grummond, *The Baratarians and the Battle of New Orleans* (Baton Rouge, La.:Louisiana State University Press, 1961), p. 5.

3. Ibid., p. 5.

4. Ibid., p. 7.

5. Ibid., p. 13.

6. W. T. Block, "The Legacy of Jean Laffite in Southwest Louisiana," *True West*, December 1979, p. 28.

7. de Grummond, p. 21.

8. Ibid., p. 42.

9. Ibid., p. 44.

10. Ibid., p. 45.

11. Leavitt <http://www.neworleansonline.com/gcno-lafitte.htm> (May 1999).

12. Block, p. 26.

13. Ibid., p. 30.

Chapter 10. Cheng I Sao

1. Jo Stanley, *Bold in Her Breeches: Women Pirates Across the Ages* (Hammersmith, London: Harper Collins Publishers, 1995), p. 207.

2. Ulrike Klausmann, Marion Meinzerin, and Gabriel Kuhn, *Women Pirates and the Politics of the Jolly Roger* (New York: Black Rose Books, 1997), p. 37.

3. Grace Fox, *British Admirals and Chinese Pirates* (Westport, Conn.: Hyperion Press, 1940), p. 80.

4. Klausmann, Meinzerin, and Kuhn, p. 38.

5. Dian H. Murray, *Pirates of the South China Coast* (Stanford, Calif.: Stanford University Press, 1987), p. 128.

6. Klausmann, Meinzerin, and Kuhn, p. 40.

7. Murray, p. 72.

8. Klausmann, Meinzerin, and Kuhn, p. 41.

9. Jan Rogozinski, *Pirates: An A–Z Encyclopedia* (New York: Facts On File, 1995), p. 70.

10. Ibid., p. 304.

11. Ibid.

12. Murray, p. 135.

13. Klausmann, Meinzerin, and Kuhn, p. 35.

14. Ibid., p. 42.

15. Ibid., p. 43.

16. Murray, p. 143.

Further Reading

Blackwood, Gary. L., *Pirates*, (Tarrytown, NY: Marshall Cavendish Corporation, 2001).

Farman, John, *The Short & Bloody History of Pirates*, (Mineapolis, Minn.: The Lerner Publishing Group, 2002).

Hague, Michael, *The Book of Pirates*, (New York: HarperCollins Children's Book Group, 2001).

Meltzer, Milton, *Piracy and Plunder: A Murderous Business*, (New York: Penguin Putnam Books, 2001).

Netzley, Patricia D., *Pirates*, (Farmington Hills, Mich.: Gale Group, 2002).

Platt, Richard, *The Pirate*, (New York: Dorling Kindersley Publishing, Inc., 2000).

Internet Addresses

National Geographic Society: Pirates of the Whydah.
www.nationalgeographic.com/whydah/main.html

Pyrate's Providence
www.inkyfingers.com/pyrates/

Website for Exploration of Queen Anne's Revenge
www.ah.dcr.state.nc.us/qar/

Index